Patience

By Jacqueline Richards

Patience

Author: Jacqueline Richards

Illustrations: Tânia Gomes

Cover and layout: Tânia Gomes

The ability to wait for something without getting angry or upset is a valuable quality in a person. We all need to practice our patience.

This is dedicated with love to my boys, Carson (my baby bear) and Rhett (my cuddle bug).

Carson is a very curious and busy boy. He is always asking for something and wants it right away. He has trouble waiting.

One sunny afternoon Carson asked, "Mom, can I go outside and play?"

"Of course," she replied, "give me a few minutes"

"But Mom, I want to go right now, please!"

Made

♥

with
LOVE

So, his mom stopped what she was doing to open the patio door so Carson could go outside with his brother and play in the backyard.

Carson was only outside for a few minutes when he came back inside and said, "Mom, I want you to come outside too."

"Carson, I am busy right now, but I'll come out and play with you later," she said.

This did not make Carson happy. He stomped his feet and threw his toy truck on the ground.

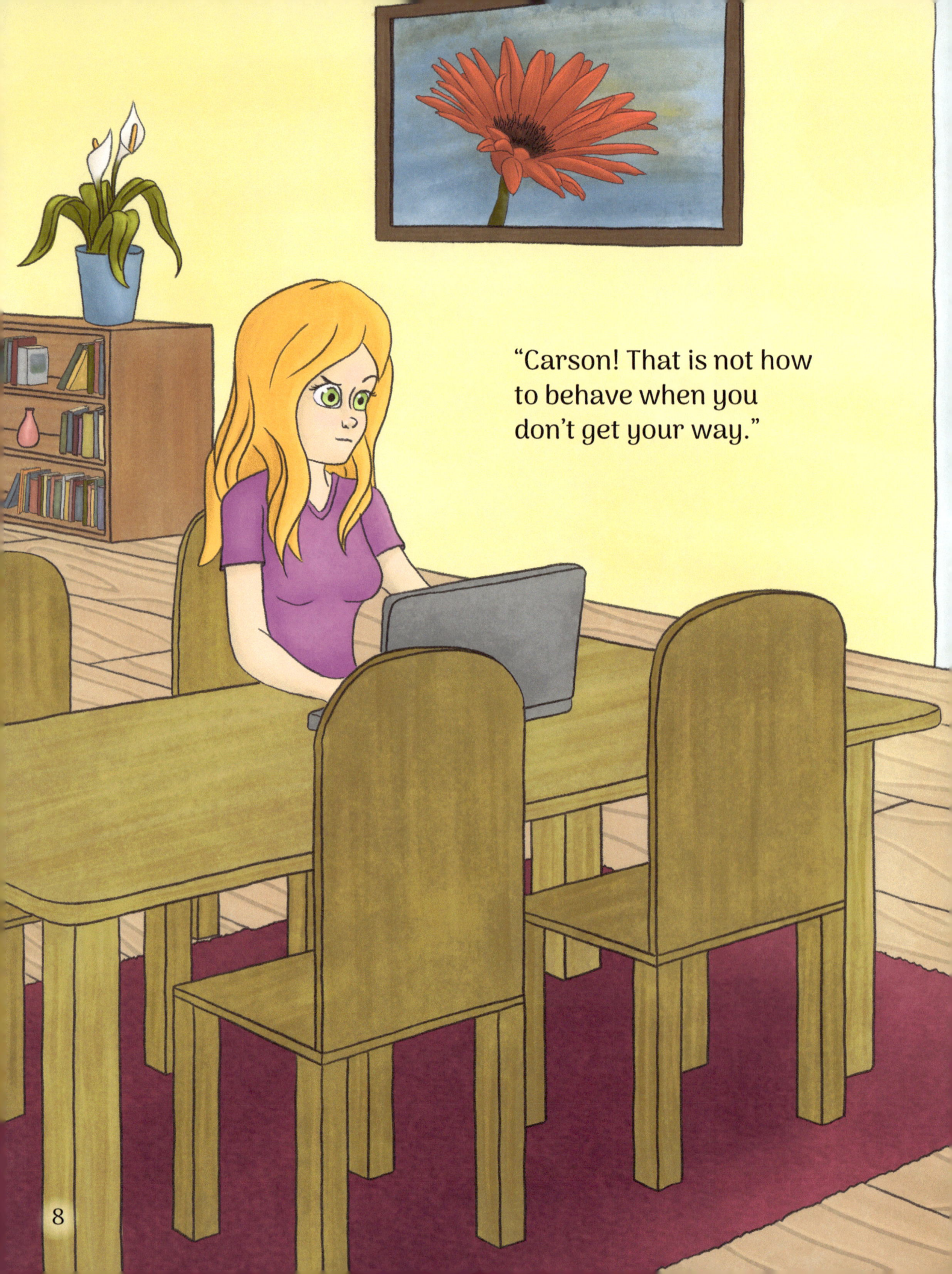

"Carson! That is not how
to behave when you
don't get your way."

"Sorry Mom," he said with his head down as he went back outside to play.

Hmmm, Carson's Mom wondered. What could she do to show Carson how to have patience?

The next day Carson, his Mom, and his brother went to get haircuts. After they were finished Carson's Mom promised to stop for a tasty treat! Everyone was very excited to go through the drive-through. "Mom, I want a milk shake!" Carson squealed with delight. "Me too, me too!" his brother yelled with excitement.

The lineup in the drive-through seemed to be taking forever and Carson's Mom started to drum her fingers on the steering wheel. She let out a big sigh and said loudly, "Ugh, what is taking so long?!"

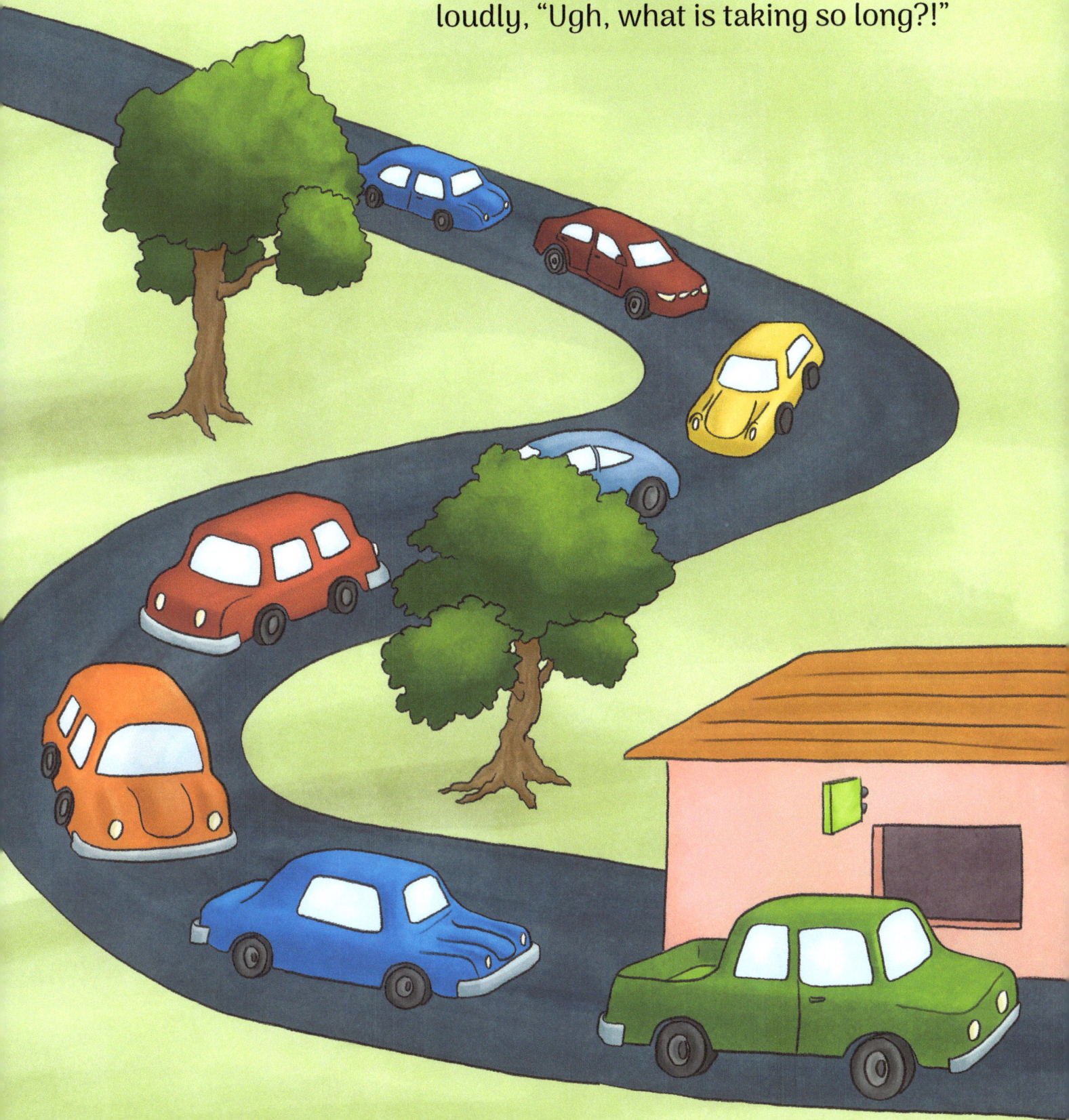

The boys chimed in, "Ya Mom, what is taking so long?"

Carson's brother started to kick his feet against the back of the seat, while Carson huffed and hawed loudly so his mother could hear.

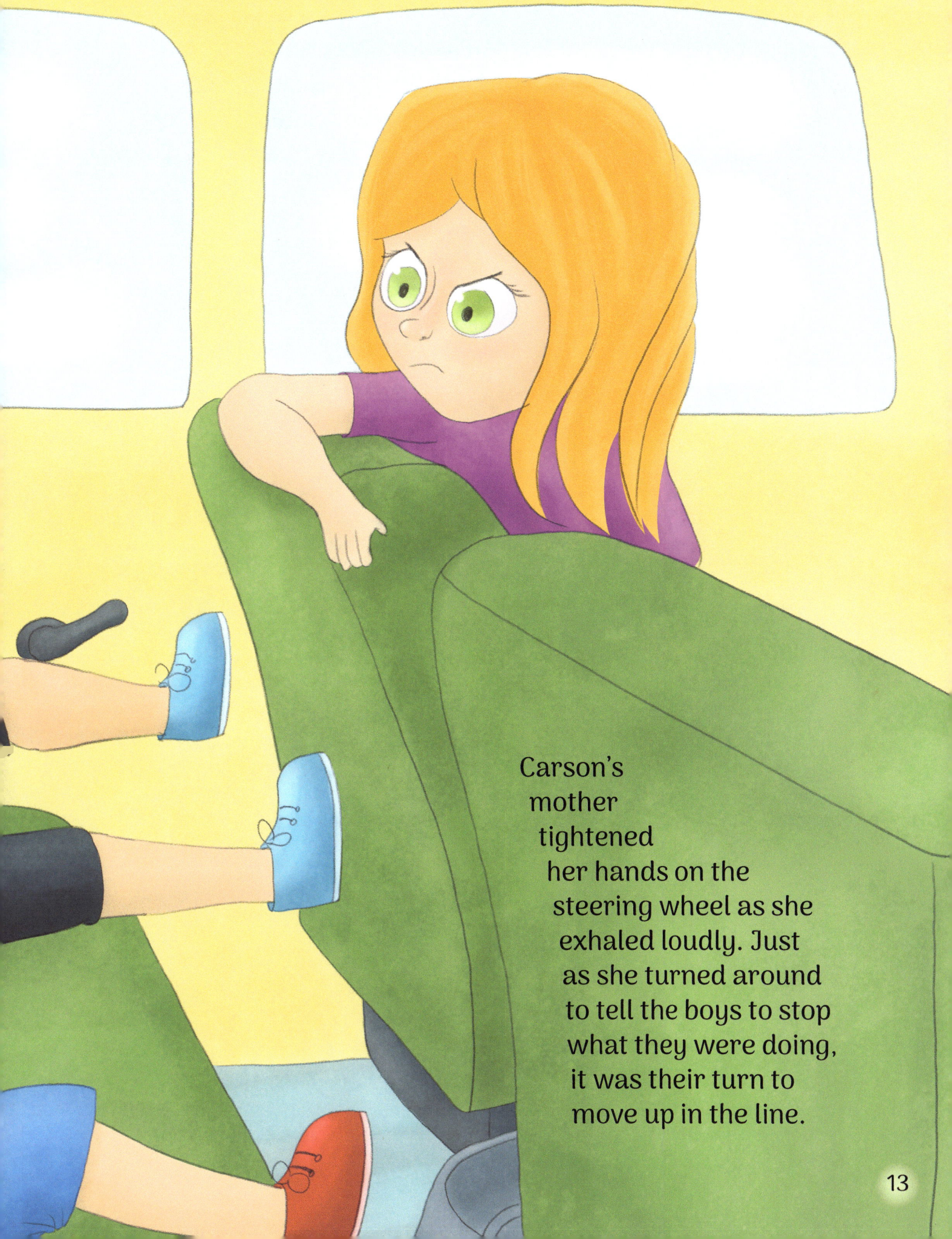

Carson's mother tightened her hands on the steering wheel as she exhaled loudly. Just as she turned around to tell the boys to stop what they were doing, it was their turn to move up in the line.

As they got to the window Carson's Mom was not happy for having to wait so long. She grabbed the drinks out of the barista's hand quickly. The barista smiled and said, "I'm sorry for the delay, we had an issue with one of our machines. Thank you for your patience."

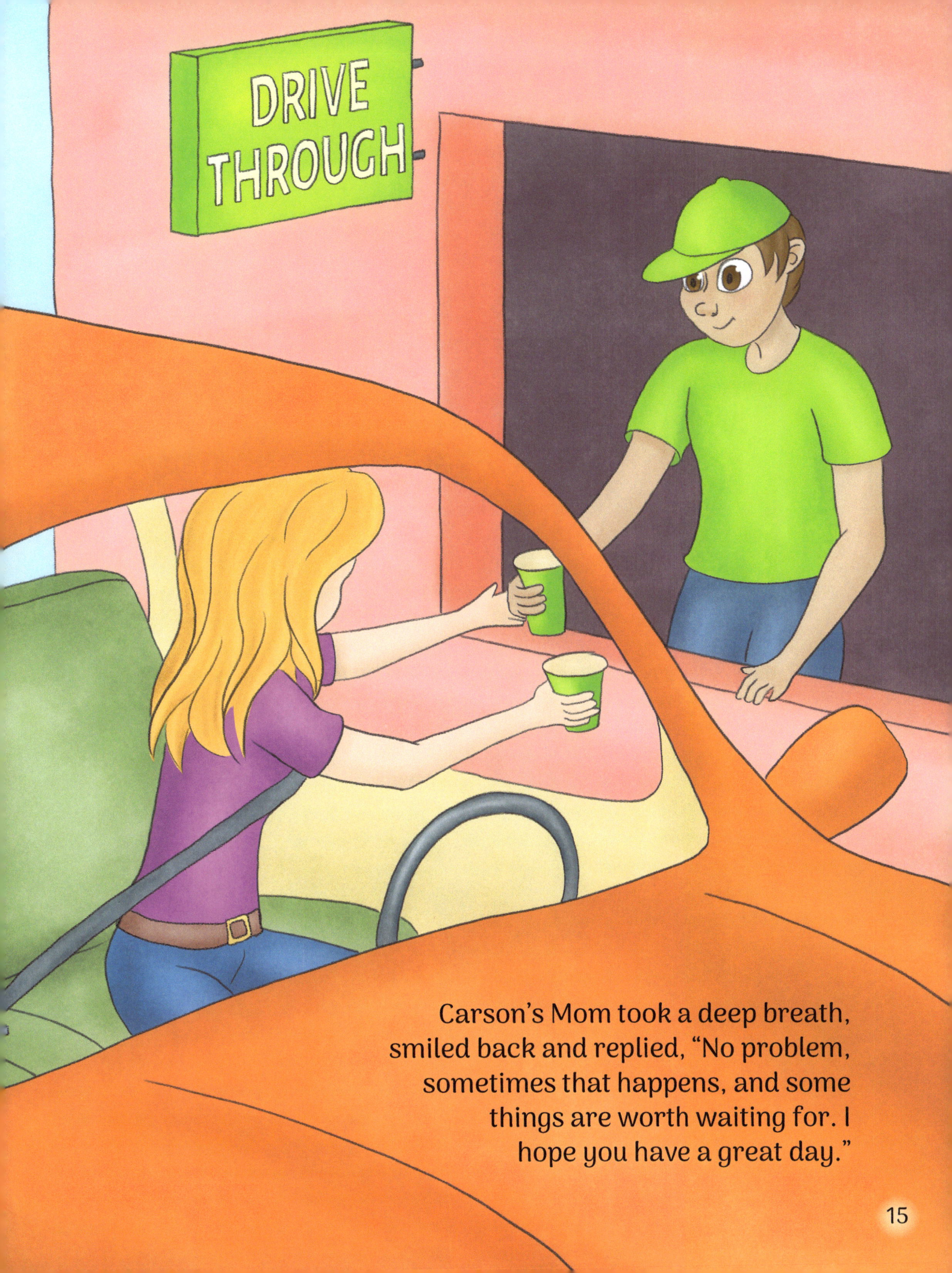

Carson's Mom took a deep breath, smiled back and replied, "No problem, sometimes that happens, and some things are worth waiting for. I hope you have a great day."

Carson's Mom handed the boys their yummy milk shakes that they had been waiting for. Suddenly Carson's mom smiled. She had a great idea.

The next day, Mom set her idea in motion.

Carson loves sour candies; they are his favourite! As she was getting the bowl of candies ready Carson was watching her and getting very excited. "Mom, are those for me? Can I have them now? I want them now, please!"

Carson's
Mom put the
bowl of sour candies in
front of him and said, "Carson,
do not touch those until I get back."
Carson did not know that his Mom was watching
him secretly to see if he would be patient and not touch
them until she returned.

Carson leaned forward, smelled the candies and even reached for them, but he did not touch them. Carson looked around for his Mom, but he couldn't see her. "Mom, Mom, Mom!" he called out. Carson couldn't take his eyes off the candies. How was his Mom going to know if he snuck just one?

He didn't want to get in trouble, so he started singing softly to himself, "Patience, patience, patience."

He looked around for his Mom again. It seemed like she was gone a long time. Carson's Mom was watching him the whole time to see if he would be patient. He was very good, even though he wanted those candies so badly! They looked so good.

Then FINALLY, she came back!

"Carson did you have any while I was gone?"

"No, Mom."

"Great job being patient, Carson! You can have some now." Carson was very excited and quickly grabbed some candies to eat.

"Carson, you did a great job showing patience and waiting before having some of your favourite candies. I'm so proud of you."

" Thanks Mom, but what is patience?" Carson asked.

"Patience means that sometimes you need to wait for things without becoming upset."

"Mom, you weren't very patient at the drive-through, then," Carson said. Carson's Mom laughed. "You are right Carson, I guess we can all learn to practice being patient."

"OK mom, I will practice being patient," he said as he wandered off singing, "Patience, patience, patience."

We all need to remember to be patient.
Did you practice your patience today?

www.ingramcontent.com/pod-product-compliance
Lightning Source LLC
LaVergne TN
LVHW072111070426
835509LV00002B/109